Restoring Our Garden of Liberty

Raising A New Generation of Patriots

Kimberly Fletcher
Marlene Peterson
Tammy Hulse

Dedicated to Dreamers

*Your homes are set upon the land a dreamer found...
[Dreamers] are the chosen few – the Blazers of the way –
who never wear doubt's bandage on their eyes – who
starve and chill and hurt, but hold to courage and to
hope, because they know that there is always proof of
truth for them who try – that only cowardice and lack of
faith can keep the seeker from his chosen goal, but if his
heart be strong and if he dream enough and dream it
hard enough, he can attain, no matter where men failed
before.*

*Walls crumble and the empires fall. The tidal wave
sweeps from the sea and tears a fortress from its rocks.
The rotting nations drop from off Time's bough, and only
things the dreamers make live on.*[1]

Gardeners of Liberty

*There is no place like Home to restore the virtues that
made this country great.*

*It is easier to build strong
children than to repair broken men.*
– Frederick Douglass

While speaking about those who influenced his life,
George Washington said, "My mother was the most
beautiful woman I ever saw. All I am I owe to my
mother. I attribute all my success in life to the moral,
intellectual and physical education I received from her."
Across the ocean in another country, Napoleon
Bonaparte said, "Let France have good mothers and she
will have good sons." The leaders of yesterday honored
and revered mothers. Many generations ago, our society
looked upon mothers as fulfilling vital and dignified
roles in the development of the nation's citizenry and
society. The home and family was viewed as the
fundamental unit of society and the strength of the

family was considered a critical component to the strength of a nation.

Here in America, a term was created to describe mothers who dedicated their time and energy to the creation of the home. The term was *homemaker*. This term was held in high esteem and to help preserve the vital arts and skills of homemaking, the public schools provided required courses in some of the homemaking arts. But times have changed and over the course of the past fifty years, there has been a vicious attack on the home, family and the homemaker.

The destroyers of liberty and virtue recognized long ago the powerful influence of mothers and homemakers. They have been working for years, desperately trying to diminish a mother's influence by deceiving, distracting, and discrediting the homemaker. Many of the home arts education courses have been abolished from the schools and individuals are encouraged in pursuits that take them away from the home and family. For many, the term "home" merely refers to a place to eat and sleep and the "homemaker" is looked upon simply as a maid, cook and child care provider. The attack on the family has been so successful that even mothers have been deceived about the influence they can have on their own children.

The widow of Egyptian president Anwar Sadat attended a luncheon not long after a mass shooting in a U.S. High School. As the conversation turned to this horrifying event, one man suggested the problem was with the failure of law enforcement agencies. Mrs. Sadat immediately countered, "No, the problem is with our homes. Too many mothers have abdicated responsibility for teaching their children what is right. What happens in society all begins with mothers."[2]

A woman's influence is a powerful thing. One prominent religious leader called women "the one bright shining hope in a world that is marching toward self-destruction." Today, America is facing disturbing challenges – our economy teeters on the verge of collapse, loud voices are being raised in contentious rhetoric, and stories of shocking violence scroll across our TV screens on a daily basis. Students of history understand the cycles of civilization and recognize these signs of a civilization in decline. Now, more than ever, we need mothers and homemakers to stand up and demonstrate the tremendous influence they can have on their family and society.

There is no place like *Home* to restore the virtues that made this country great. There is no place like *Home* to inspire greatness in tomorrow's leaders. One of our objectives at Homemakers for America is to restore the role of *homemaker* to its rightful place of honor and dignity. Our members will notice a slight change in the spelling of homemaker to reflect the change that must take place within the American home. Our homes must be transformed from a "dwelling place" to a "growing place" and the maker of the home must be elevated from maid and cook to creator and nurturer. The term "home" becomes "<u>H</u>ome" when it encompasses a nurturing, inspiring environment where family members can achieve their full potential. The phrase "maker of the home" becomes "<u>M</u>aker of the Home" when mothers become creators of an environment that will nurture, protect, educate, and inspire family members. Thus, the new spelling for our organization will be HomeMakers for America.

The HomeMaker is a nurturer. To nurture means to cultivate, to care for and to make grow. Just as a master gardener creates an ideal environment for plants to grow, the HomeMaker creates the home environment that allows the inherent potential of all family members to be achieved. HomeMaking is vital and dignified. It requires organization, patience, love and work. We have adopted the companion name of *Gardeners of Liberty* to serve as a constant reminder of the vital roles of creation and nurturing that belong to the HomeMaker.

A nurturing environment includes opportunity for physical, emotional, spiritual, and intellectual growth and achievement. We recognize that this can feel like a daunting and overwhelming task to women; therefore, our second objective at HomeMakers for America is to provide education, support and encouragement for women who are looking for help in their role of HomeMaker. We invite women and men across the country to join us as we discard the false notions of recent past generations and restore the Mother and HomeMaker to the place of honor and dignity it deserves.

"We fancy that God can only manage his world with battalions, when all the while he is doing it by beautiful babies. When a wrong wants righting, or a truth needs preaching or a continent needs opening, God sends a baby into the world...perhaps in a simple home and of some obscure mother. And then God puts the idea into the mother's heart, and she puts it into the baby's mind. And then God waits. The greatest forces in the world are not the earthquakes and thunderbolts. The greatest forces in the world are babies."[3]

Mothers, the future of America is in our hands. God has put the idea in our hearts. And now . . . God waits.

Our Garden of Liberty

*I know no safe depository of the ultimate powers of society
but the people themselves; and if we think them not
enlightened enough to exercise their control with a wholesome
discretion, the remedy is not to take it from them, but to
inform their discretion by education.
This is the true corrective of abuses of constitutional power."*
                                    – Thomas Jefferson

My* mother had a big, beautiful garden. The walkway leading down to it was lined with fruit trees of every kind – apple, pear, apricot, plum, cherry, peach and nectarine. The garden itself was a masterpiece – every vegetable you can imagine with strawberries growing in carefully painted boxes and the whole garden was bordered by a massive row of raspberries. Sprinkled throughout were splashes of golden marigold, pale pink peonies and purpose cosmos.

* Marlene

Our Garden of Liberty

My children were small when my mother had this garden and they loved to play in it. They chased butterflies and danced on the little bridge that crossed the creek on the backside of the property. Many evenings I stood at the top of the hill and watched the sun set behind them, taking in the lilac and honeysuckle scented breezes while they gathered baskets full of big, juicy blackberries, raspberries and strawberries. It was as close to a piece of heaven on earth as I can think of.

As my mother got older, she needed to move to a smaller place and it was my good fortune to inherit this magnificent garden. I excitedly looked forward to carrying on the tradition. Maybe I should mention, though, that my mother had grown up on a farm in Idaho. I was a California city girl. We had a swimming pool in our back yard, not a garden. Why I thought I could step into that garden and instinctively know how to take care of it makes no sense to me today. At the time, I couldn't see any problems.

Our Garden of Liberty

That first spring, my husband and I eagerly picked out the packets of seeds and took our kids down to the garden to plant them. We felt so proud of ourselves as we stepped back and dreamed of the great harvest ahead but seemingly overnight, we found ourselves facing the biggest crop of weeds you've ever seen. We couldn't even tell the weeds from the plants. Nothing had prepared us for the amount of time and work it was going to take to get on top of them. And we never did.

As the season wore on, I noticed the leaves on the raspberry plants were starting to curl and wither, and then the plants started to die. We cut them all down, hoping they'd grow back the next spring. They didn't.

The strawberries stopped producing fruit, the apples had worms in them, and our entire cherry crop was carried away by the birds who mockingly spit the pits back at us.

Realizing we had overestimated ourselves, the next year we decided to focus on one crop. So we went out and bought every variety of tomato plant we could find – seventy-two plants in all. We watered them, and weeded them and caged them and then one glorious day we had a bonanza harvest of tomatoes. We picked boxes and boxes of them. We gave them to our neighbors and friends. We had tomatoes with every meal. We made salsa and spaghetti sauce, but we still we found ourselves with boxes and boxes of tomatoes . . . rotting in our patio. After a while, there was nothing we could do but take them out to the field and dump them.

Now, I'm sure you're thinking what a dope I was. Why on earth did I not can them? The simple fact was, I didn't know how.

The next year, we planted two zucchini plants. And then after that, it was just easier and cheaper to buy all our produce at the store.

Within a few, short seasons, my mother's beautiful garden was overrun and choked with weeds. I had completely ruined it – certainly not out of willfulness but out of sheer ignorance. Now, no one would ever say the garden had failed. Clearly, the fault was with the hands to which the garden had been entrusted. I simply had no clue how to take care of it or how to make good use of the fruits of that labor.

There are those today who say our Garden of Liberty has failed – the American experiment in self-government doesn't work. They even go so far as to say that our "sweet land of liberty" never even existed. These "enlightened" ones tell us there's nothing left to do but plow under the garden, and pour a nice slab of cement over it and plant a Walmart on top, because, as we all know, you can get everything you need at Walmart.

But I can tell you from my own experience, that even though the strawberries I buy from a store may provide many of the nutritional requirements my body needs to survive, I have never tasted a store-bought strawberry that came anywhere close to tasting as sweet

Our Garden of Liberty

as the strawberries from my mother's garden. And I, for one, am not ready to settle.

And so I have been doing what I should have done with my mother's garden – I've spent the last several years digging up and brushing off the gardener's manuals. Fortunately for us, those who gave us our Republic left us with detailed notes and advice. They told us what pests and bugs to be on guard against. They described the symptoms of disease and how to treat it before it caused too much damage.

What I noticed most in their writings was their focus on soil preparation. They knew that the secret behind the miracle of America had everything to do with the hearts and character of her citizens. Without adequate soil preparation, the garden wouldn't grow, so one of their first orders of business was to establish common schools for the purpose of training up the next generation of gardeners for the Republic they had labored so hard to establish.

Our Garden of Liberty

I've read some of the school laws and statutes of many of these early schools. Their national standards looked a bit different than ours. Their instructional focus was on "principles of piety, justice, and a sacred regard to truth, love to their country, humanity and universal benevolence, sobriety, industry and frugality, chastity, moderation, and temperance, and those other virtues which are the ornament of human society and the basis upon which a republican constitution is founded."[4] Their stated outcome was "to lead their pupils into a clear understanding of the tendency of the above-mentioned virtues, to preserve and perfect a republican constitution, and secure the blessings of liberty, as well as to promote their future happiness."[5]

When was the last time you heard anyone bring up any of these concerns when we talk about problems with education today? Somewhere along the way it seems our schools stopped teaching our children to tend and grow their own gardens of happiness and, instead, started producing skilled laborers to work in someone else's garden.

Our Garden of Liberty

Another common thread of instruction that ran through all their writings was the necessity of an open Bible because the Bible was the rock upon which everything was built. They warned that you may as well plant a seed in air and expect it to grow as ignore the Bible and expect America to thrive. After all, a people who knew that their inalienable rights were endowed by their Creator would never allow an intruder to step in and take those rights away. The Bible was the one book with the power to unite a people because no one group could claim ownership of it. Its universal message of the fatherhood of God and the brotherhood of man touched hearts across nationalities and across denominations. The Bible was the key to self-government. They gravely warned that if it was ignored or rejected, "our expiring anguish will surpass that of any nation that ever lived." A recent survey indicates that the average American owns three copies of the Bible, but doesn't read any of them. Are we starting to feel a bit of that "expiring anguish"?

Our Garden of Liberty

I'm afraid we've really mucked things up. Our beautiful Garden of Liberty is overrun and choked with weeds of debt, corruption and greed. We have worms in our apples and boxes of tomatoes rotting in the patio. But I'll tell you why I still have hope.

I have hope because I believe in a liberty loving God who has the power to make things right. He knows better than to hand over the rare and prized gift of liberty to a people who don't know how to take care of it or how to make good use of the inevitable bounteous harvest of prosperity that always accompanies true liberty. To place liberty in the hands of such a people is as much a waste as my mother turning her garden over to me. But just as soon as He finds a people who are prepared — who have diligently studied the gardeners' manuals and who value the gift so much that they would pledge their lives, their fortunes and their sacred honor to possess it, to that people — He promises to stand guard over them as they labor. For them, He will turn the soil over if needs be and prepare it for a new planting — just as He did with our Founding Fathers.

Our Garden of Liberty

I moved away from my mother's garden a long time ago. I feel so badly that I ruined it. I have the same pangs of regret when I read the stories of the sacrifices and struggles of our patriot mothers and fathers and think of what we've done to the beautiful Republic they left us. While there is nothing I can do to reclaim my mother's garden, there's a lot I can do as a laborer of freedom. Yes, elections and policies are important, but it turns out most of the real work of a Republic is done at home and involves character and heart. I now understand that the lessons and principles of liberty do not come instinctively to us or our children; we have to be willing to make time to learn and teach them. And anyone who believes we can move the cause of freedom forward without the Hand of Divine Providence should try gardening without sunshine.

America's Garden of Liberty is not dead, but it has been sorely neglected. We are at risk of losing it altogether. We at HomeMakers for America believe it's worth every effort to restore it for our children and our children's children. Do you?

Our Garden of Liberty

* * * * * * * * * * * *

"If the experiment of government by the people is to be successful, it is you and such as you who must make it so. The future of the Republic must lie in the hands of the men and women of culture and intelligence, of self-control and of self-resource, capable of taking care of themselves and of helping others. If it falls <u>not</u> into such hands, the republic will have no future.....The problem of life is not to make life easier, but to make men stronger, so that no problem shall be beyond their solution...The remedy for oppression is to bring in better men who cannot be oppressed."[6]

Building stronger men and women who cannot be oppressed is a job for mothers. In the pages that follow, we will share with you ideas for accomplishing this vital task. Growing enlightened, educated and empowered citizens is the true restorative work in a Garden of Liberty.

Wisdom is knowing what to do next.
Virtue is doing it.[7]

Restorative Garden Work
Step One: Cultivate the Soil
with Faith

It is when people forget God that
tyrants forge their chains.
– Patrick Henry

What comes from heaven to heaven by nature clings,
And if dissevered thence, its course is short.
– Wordsworth

My* dad loved to plant flowers in our back yard. I enjoyed learning their names – hydrangea, hollyhocks and camellias. When I was just 3 or 4 years old, I went out to help him one day. I saw a little packet of seeds on the ground and found a hard piece of dirt where I sprinkled a few seeds and scratched a little bit of dirt over them. He watched what I was doing and then he

*Marlene

took me by the hand and led me to a little two foot square patch of dirt by the garage where he dug the shovel in deep, turning the soil over while adding a mixture which I was too young to know was fertilizer. He then had me sprinkle in my seeds.

He didn't have to use words to teach me the lesson of that summer as I watched the plants in the cultivated soil produce profuse blooms of brilliant orange all summer long while my seeds planted in the hard dirt never grew.

Likewise, the condition of the soil determines the success of a Garden of Liberty. Unfortunately, our soil has become hard and terribly depleted. Gardeners of Liberty first need to prepare and condition the soil to create an atmosphere where the seeds of true freedom can grow.

Hearts are softened as we recognize the reality of God and our dependence on Him. "In God We Trust" can be found on all American currency. Not only should these words remain engraved on our coins, but they should also be embedded into the hearts of our citizens as we turn the soil in preparation for planting. Faith in God is where it all begins, and with this faith, minds and hearts are open to divine instruction and guidance.

The faith of a mother will leave deep impressions upon the hearts of her children. The power of faith comes from a firm and accurate belief in God. It is not a mere fleeting hope of God's existence but an assurance of His reality that moves mothers to act.

It was by faith that Abigail Adams courageously cared for her young family alone, while her husband was away serving his country. It was by faith that the wives of the signers of the Declaration of Independence sacrificed and stood by their husbands, placing their own lives, fortunes and sacred honors on the line as well.

It was by faith that Martha Washington served the soldiers in her husband's winter encampments. It was Martha's cheerful and optimistic nature that brought great comfort to her husband and his men as she repaired their clothing, darned their socks and visited with the soldiers, especially those who were sick or wounded.

It was by faith that George Washington led a rag-tag army through an eight-year war against the greatest army on earth into a glorious victory that brought American independence.

It was by faith that Abraham Lincoln turned to God during the battle of Gettysburg and pled for victory. He made a vow that if God would stand by the boys at Gettysburg that he, Abraham Lincoln, would stand by God.

We need not fear as long as we have the power of faith, for 'with God, nothing shall be impossible.'

It was the faith of our Fathers that brought them to America. These early Pilgrims carried with them a significant Book – a book which even the right to read was bought with a dear price. Readers had been burned with copies round their necks. Husbands had been made to witness against their wives, and children were forced to light the death-fires of their parents. Possessors of the banned book had been hunted down as if they were wild beasts. Considerable sums of money had been paid for the privilege of reading even a few sheets of the manuscript. A farmer might have given up a load of hay for permission to read it for even one hour a day.

This book, for which people risked their lives, is the same book that today the average American today owns three copies of, but rarely reads.

What power did this Book hold over the hearts of men that would make rulers fear? It's the same power feared by tyrants today, so they create godless societies to hold on to their control over the lives of people. A people of faith walk in trust and confidence in a Higher Power. They allow no earthly ruler to rule over them.

Step One: Cultivate the Soil

They hold dear their inalienable rights granted by their Creator.

The Bible speaks directly from God to the heart. He has no need for an interpreter or a middleman. Through its words, we feel the love of a Father and a purpose for our existence. While statistics tell us many of our youth are leaving organized religion, they also tell us their quest for spirituality and meaning remains high. We are living in the day described by the prophet Amos: "Behold, the days come , saith the Lord God, that I will send a famine in the land, not a famine of bread, nor a thirst for water, but of hearing the words of the Lord; And they shall wander from sea to sea, and from the north even to the east, they shall run to and fro to seek the word of the Lord, and shall not find it. In that day shall the fair virgins and young men faint for thirst."[8]

Mothers are in a unique position to quench that thirst.

Restorative Garden Work

France has tried experiments in secularism. In 1878, when France was still a young Republic, the socialist party sought to banish God from "all the thoughts" of the nation by passing a law which secularized the common schools. For the next ten years, they used a purposefully prepared series of textbooks in all grade levels to teach morals while carefully omitting any reference to religion.

The next census revealed an appalling increase in juvenile crime, especially child suicide. The ten years created such a pervasive pessimism among the children that they found goodness not worth seeking and life not worth living.

The French government hired a 'serious freethinker' to study the problem. In the resulting book, *Crime and the School,* he traced the evil to one cause: "the profound soul-discouragement of the child who knew not God".[9]

Years earlier, Napoleon had reflected, "...if there had been no God it would be necessary to invent one."

Step One: Cultivate the Soil

We tell our schoolchildren the stories of the Greek and Roman gods who acted so mischievously towards humans, yet we refuse to tell them the stories of a Hebrew God who loves them as their Father. Could we act more foolishly?

Our founders sternly warned us to keep religious feelings in our hearts or we would not survive as a free people. George Washington offered this counsel: "Of all the dispositions and habits which lead to political prosperity, religion and morality are indispensable supports." We are starting to feel the effects of having this support removed from our society.

There is a simple remedy – start reading the Bible every day in our homes. Read it out loud. Read it as a family. Read from the scriptures themselves, supplementing with stories shared from the heart. You may think they're beyond a child's comprehension, but that is a mistake. A child can learn multiple languages by the time he is five simply by being exposed to them. Is it not reasonable to think that a child who is immersed in the beautiful language of the King James Version of the Bible from infancy will feel comfortable and familiar with it in the same way? And long before children fully comprehend the words, they'll respond to the feelings they have while listening to words spoken by someone who loves them.

Reading the Bible together as a family would restore more power and strength to America than any other single act. Our children will once again be connected to a light of which millions of people from nations throughout the world, across the span of hundreds and thousands of years can attest; a light that has comforted weary hearts, guided explorers, and inspired kings. To read the words of the Bible, pure and undiluted, is to share the same experience as the greatest minds that have ever lived.

The Bible belongs to all of us, Methodist and Baptist, Mormon and Presbyterian, Catholic and Jew. It is the one book capable of uniting us as a people because no one group can claim ownership of it. Its marvel is that it is not the work of one man, such as the writings of Confucius or the words of Mohammed, but a collection of writings over hundreds of years from prophets, herdsmen, kings, physicians, tax collectors, and fishermen, all being acted upon by the same sublime Spirit of Truth and delivering the same hopeful message: that life has purpose and meaning and there is a guiding power. We are not left alone to muddle our way through.

Its universal message of the fatherhood of God and the brotherhood of man touches the hearts of the poor and the rich, the scholar and the unlearned, those in captivity and those who are free. Its wisdom is valued by the Hindu, the Muslim and even the atheist. It needs no commentary to be understood. It offers ideas so simple a little child can grasp them, and yet scholars can spend a lifetime attempting to uncover the depth of their meaning. One simple phrase from its pages, on many occasions, has changed the course of a life and even the course of nations.

Restorative Garden Work

The most deeply moving music that has ever been composed, the most inspiring art that has ever been painted, and the most exquisite words that have ever been written have found their inspiration in the Bible.

As Lincoln exclaimed, the Bible is simply the greatest gift God has given to mankind.

Serious Gardeners of Liberty cannot ignore it.

Restorative Garden Work
Step Two: Plant Seeds of Virtue

Virtue, morality and religion.
This is the armor, my friend,
and this alone renders us invincible.
These are the tactics we should study.
If we lose these, we are conquered, fallen indeed....
– Patrick Henry

The only foundation of a free Constitution,
is pure Virtue, and if this cannot be inspired into our People,
in a greater Measure than they have it now,
they may change their Rulers, and the forms
of Government, but they will not obtain a lasting Liberty.
– John Adams

If you want to grow a cantaloupe, you have to plant a cantaloupe seed. If you want to grow a zucchini, you first have to plant a zucchini seed. Neither the cantaloupe nor the zucchini will one day magically

29

appear in the garden where a seed has not first been planted. You also can't plant a zucchini seed and expect a cantaloupe to grow. It's the law of the harvest. We reap what we sow.

While not every seed that is planted will sprout, it is guaranteed that you will never get fruit from a seed that is never planted.

We hear many voices today crying out for smaller government and getting back to the Constitution, yet we hear little of the other side of the equation that demands that we be a people who are *capable* of living under a limited government. Only a people who can govern themselves will be able to sustain liberty. Virtue is moral excellence and is a requirement of a free people.

Benjamin Franklin warned, "Only a virtuous people are capable of freedom. As nations become more corrupt and vicious, they have more need of masters."

Step Two: Plant Seeds of Virtue

A Gardener of Liberty plants seeds of virtue in young hearts where they can take root and grow.

Virtues are certain attributes that are most likely to ensure we will not just survive; we will thrive. They are key to meaningful relationships, individual greatness and are connected to our ultimate happiness. Thomas Jefferson observed, "Without virtue, happiness cannot be." Benjamin Franklin lived his life around 13 virtues: temperance, silence, order, resolution, frugality, industry, sincerity, justice, moderation, cleanliness, tranquility, chastity and humility. America's early common schools promoted: principles of piety, justice, a sacred regard to truth, love to their country, humanity and universal benevolence, sobriety, industry and frugality, chastity, moderation and temperance. How many of us even know what those words mean anymore? We might add to the list such traits as honesty, courage, loyalty, gratitude and patience.

A virtuous life cannot be forced on anyone – it must be chosen by individual hearts. "Goodness" cannot be legislated, although plenty of people have tried with disastrous results. Parents can't 'require' moral excellence of their children. Children may comply outwardly for a time, but it won't last until they have made an inward choice.

There is an ageless method of seed planting that is largely lost to today's parents. It is how a free people instill virtue without force. This ageless proven method of planting virtue in our children is to wrap the trait we hope to develop inside a story. You find evidence of this method in cultures around the world and throughout history. The Native Americans used it and a study of their culture reveals a people of valor, strong moral courage and a keen sensitivity to the Spirit. The Ancient Greeks used it. The Hebrews relied upon it. Through this simple method between parent and child, they kept a longing for their homeland alive for over 1800 years even though they were scattered clear across the world. America saw a revival of this seed-planting method in the early 1900's among mothers and teachers of young children. While we may not have scientific data to prove a connection, we know the 'Greatest Generation' followed. Re-learning this ancient art could produce an even greater generation.

Stories are the means by which ideas are carried into the heart. Information and facts remain in the mind where we don't care about them. It's their connection to the heart that makes stories the most powerful gardening tool we have.

Jesus relied upon stories. Consider that he only had about three years to establish a faith that would transform the world, yet he chose to use his time telling stories. The fact that Jesus' priority was storytelling should give us a good sense of its power.

We're not talking about reading stories together, although there is great value in doing that. We're talking about putting the book down, holding our children in our arms, and telling them a story *by heart*. Oh, the wonderful, far-reaching opportunity held in such moments as these! When the lights are low and your child is in a quiet, receptive mood, the stories told to him will never be forgotten and their influence will follow him the rest of his life. Storytelling transforms a mother from an authority figure to a trusted guide and confidante. Sharing stories from the heart weaves hearts together and creates bonds that are nearly impossible to break.

Our children's ability to maintain hope during trying times is in direct proportion to how deep and how wide their reservoir of stories is. A heart stocked full of stories provides solutions to draw from for every problem it may face. Stories keep hearts from failing.

Stories have the ability to make 'virtue' look appealing and increases the likelihood of adapting that attribute or trait. How do we expect our kids to be 'good' if we don't show them what 'good' looks like?

My* son-in-law recently deployed overseas with the military for a year and I went with my little

*Marlene

granddaughters to see him off. Six-year-old Kayleigh had been dreading the moment because she adores her father. She hugged him tight and when the time came for him to board the bus, she could no longer hold back the tears and I watched her sob as though her heart would break. Her little shoulders heaved as she tried to deal with her raw emotions.

I quietly knelt down on the ground next to her, put my arms around her and whispered a simple little story in her ear. I told her of another little girl whose daddy went off to war. She cried when he left and missed him so much that she didn't know what she was going to do. But then she thought to herself how much her Daddy loved America. She was so proud of him, that everywhere she went she told people that her daddy was a soldier. I told her how brave this little girl was. It was hard to have him gone, but one day he came home and hugged her and she was so happy.

There really wasn't much to the story, but somehow it gave Kayleigh something to hold on to. She wiped the tears from her eyes, stood up tall and waved to him until the bus drove off. I watched her over the next couple of days as she shared with the grownups we came in contact with that her daddy was a soldier. They always responded with such warmth and gratitude that soon she didn't need to say it anymore.

Telling her this little story accomplished two things. First, she gained the assurance she wasn't alone; it provided her a shared experience. Secondly, it gave her a way through.

Never underestimate the power of a story.

A certain man had a friend who was a beekeeper. One day when he came to visit, he found his friend in deep despair. "I'm ruined. All my honey is bitter. What am I going to do?" The man suggested they get up early the next morning and follow the swarm of bees to see what they were feeding on, which they did. They were led to an old abandoned factory where they found barrels of rotting, gooey, icky syrups from which the bees were filling up their little pollen sacs and flying back to the hive.

The man kindly suggested, "Change what your bees are feeding on and you'll change the quality of your honey."

What stories are our kids feeding on? If we hope to raise a virtuous generation, our path is clear. Stories of virtue are in short supply today. We desperately need heart-touching soul-penetrating stories. We may have to rely on the stories of yesteryear for a while – a time when writers purposefully wrote to show what 'good' looks like. The storytellers of the early 1900's left us not only lessons in the art of storytelling but also the keys to a literal treasure chest of golden stories to tell – noble acts of great men and women; epic heroes and knights from the age of chivalry; imaginative fairy tales; stories told in paintings, music and nature; stories of history; stories that develop character. We will share them with you.

Restorative Garden Work

As we pay attention to the stories our children are feeding on, we will see an increase of virtue start to manifest itself. The word 'virtue' is defined as 'strength' and 'power' and has a quality to it which implies its ability to 'produce effects on other bodies'.

Virtue is accompanied by a power that is far greater than the armies of nations. History has demonstrated this truth. Adolf Hitler had assembled a military force that seemed unbeatable; yet he could not defeat a tiny island across the English Channel because of the virtue and faith of Winston Churchill. This one man unified the will of the people through principles of freedom and selfless sacrifice.

We find another example in Mahatma Gandhi, a ninety-pound man who single handedly overcame the vast British Empire that ruled two-thirds of the face of the globe. Gandhi's success is attributed to his ability to stand for principle: the intrinsic dignity of man and his right to freedom, sovereignty, and self-determination. Gandhi's faith was based on the fact that such rights are

Step Two: Plant Seeds of Virtue

bestowed upon man by virtue of the divinity of his creation and not to be granted by any earthly power.

It was the virtue of one man, George Washington, that kept the fire of liberty burning in hearts when the outcome looked so bleak and impossible.

A mother clothed with virtue will exercise the same power.

<u>One</u> man or woman of virtue can lift and influence an entire nation. Imagine the power if we, as mothers, could grow an entire generation of men and women of virtue.

Let the storytelling begin!

> *Righteousness exalteth a nation.*
> Proverbs 14:34

Restorative Garden Work
Step Three: Water and Tend the Plants with Patriotism and Knowledge

Freedom has its life in the hearts, the actions,
the spirit of men and so it must be
daily earned and refreshed else
like a flower cut from its life-giving
roots, it will wither and die.
– Dwight D. Eisenhower

...the salvation of this great republic
will depend upon your unselfish patriotism.
– George Washington

After the soil has been turned over and fertilized and the seeds have been planted, imagine what the garden would look like if it were then left to itself. Tender plants in a Garden of Liberty need to be watered often with a correct knowledge of our heritage and true principles of liberty. False notions must be weeded out.

Patriotism is a matter of the heart. It grows out of knowledge – to know America is to love her – and as has been said, is the "noblest passion that animates a citizen." A people who do not love their country will neither serve nor fight for her. Thomas Jefferson said, ". . . a government is like everything else: to preserve it, we must love it . . ."

A lack of patriotism today, as expressed in the following examples from some of our young people, stands as one of our greatest threats to freedom:

A university student in a Stanford University research study on U. S. Citizenship said, "Being American is not really special. I don't find being an American citizen very important."

Restorative Garden Work

In a young man's blog written around the 4th of July, he said he was planning on eating at the barbeque and he might be able to be talked into the fireworks, but don't talk to him about patriotism. He asked how you love a country that goes to war and kills innocent men, women and children or that practically exterminated one race of people, enslaved another and even denied her own women their rights. He questioned what there was about America to deserve his patriotism.

A Junior High class in Virginia was given an assignment to write an essay on why they loved America. Not one student came up with a single reason.

Expressions of patriotism are at an all-time low. Many of our children no longer recite the pledge of allegiance. They don't sing the songs of our heritage – *America, America the Beautiful, the Star-Spangled Banner.* The flag is held in disrespect. Many of us of an older generation were raised on the idea that should the flag even touch the ground, it should be burned. To leave it out in the rain or through the dark night was unthinkable. When the national anthem played, we placed our hands over our hearts and either sang along or stood silent from respect. And we all knew the words.

Does patriotism really matter?

During World War I, the French bravely fought back the invading Germans for four brutal years. Twenty years later, in World War II, France fell to Nazi Germany in just six weeks. What changed?

Much of the blame was placed squarely on the shoulders of the teachers' unions who, in a spirit of pacifism and internationalism had purged all the schoolbooks of stories of the courage and self-sacrifice of their fallen heroes. Instead, the children were bombarded with stories of the horrors and the suffering of both French and German alike.[10]

How long will our battle for freedom last?

Restorative Garden Work

If we have only taught our children the mechanics of the Constitution and have failed to tell them the stories of what life looks like without freedom; if we have only taught our children the workings of our government and have failed to tell them the stories of the price that was paid to have that government; if we have failed to tell them the stories of what made America the light and hope of the world, then our battle for freedom will not last long enough.

If our children don't love America, it's because *we* have not given them the reasons to love her. They don't understand that our system of government under the Constitution is the best system of government the world has ever seen.

Karl Marx warned, "A people without a heritage are easily persuaded."

When a nation is in chaos and has lost its identity, it's the storyteller who resets the course. Stories can heal our nation. Without a story, we don't *have* a nation.

Step Three: Water & Tend the Plants

Stories of our shared heritage unite hearts, and it's the uniting of hearts that gives us the strength and courage to push through hard times. A single twig is easily broken, but what happens when you band a dozen twigs together?

The tiny Eastern European country of Estonia showed to the world what happens. They had been under Communist rule for fifty years, but the stories and songs of their heritage had been planted deep within their hearts. For five years, beginning in the late 1980's, they systematically and repeatedly gathered in public places to sing their forbidden patriotic songs.

If you ever saw the scene in *Casablanca* where the French patrons sang La Marseillaise in defiance of the Germans and then multiply this scene by thousands, you begin to get a sense of the force behind the "Singing Revolution".

Restorative Garden Work

In the end, the Communists could not remain in power against a hundred thousand voices united in a song of the heart. They withdrew without shedding a single drop of blood.

You cannot defeat a singing nation.[11]

It is time for a rebirth of Patriotism. There is no place like home to instill Patriotism in the next generation.

This is not a job for the hired help.

How little do my countrymen know what precious blessings
they are in possession of, and which no other people
on earth enjoy!
– Thomas Jefferson

Making Good Use of the Harvest

*A desire and a feeling for beauty
are the surest guardians of survival.*
– Hugh Nibley

After we have cultivated the soil with faith, planted seeds of virtue and watered and tended the emerging plants with knowledge and truth, we can expect a bounteous harvest of liberty. A free people are always blessed with great prosperity and so one more task remains for Gardeners of Liberty – teaching and preparing our children to make good use of the harvest so that we have no tomatoes rotting in the patio.

Materialism has taken over our Garden of Liberty with its accompanying companions, greed and corruption. The culminating event of a year's hard labor seems to be the big after Thanksgiving Christmas sales. Even our education system's focus is on making a living, not making a life.

Making Good Use of the Harvest

Is that really the best use of freedom? John Adams had in mind a different ideal: "I must study politics and war, that my sons may have liberty to study mathematics and philosophy, geography, natural history and naval architecture, navigation, commerce, and agriculture, in order to give their children a right to study painting, poetry, music, architecture, statuary, tapestry and porcelain."

Although "stuff" makes our lives comfortable, we have the enviable opportunity to climb to higher places. It has been said that the reason many of our fairy tales have lasted for hundreds of years is because they are simply a kernel of Truth with a story wrapped around it. Consider the message of Sleeping Beauty to us as told in Walt Disney's film adaptation. In the story, Beauty had gone to sleep, and when she fell asleep, the entire kingdom became lifeless and colorless. Soon noxious briers and thorns and tangled vines grew around the sleeping kingdom. Prince Philip valiantly drew his sword of truth and protected himself with his shield of righteousness to make his way through the tangled mess and fight the evil Maleficent. But that isn't what brought the kingdom back to life – the thing that brought the kingdom back to life was his love of Beauty. When Beauty received true love's *first* kiss, Beauty awoke and the kingdom gloriously sprang to life.

The privilege of teaching our children a love of Beauty falls on this generation of mothers. Will we step up to the opportunity? Never before in the history of the world has a group of mothers had more labor saving devices that can potentially free up the time to engage in such a luxurious course of study with their children. Our primary concern no longer has to be fighting off starvation. And, oh, the resources we have at our fingertips! We can access great works of art right in our homes that previously could only be viewed by the rich and elite who could afford to travel the world and visit great museums. Our homes can be filled with beautiful symphonies of music that used to be reserved for royalty. All the exquisite and ennobling words of the poets and the great thinkers and writers that have traveled through hundreds, and even thousands of years of history, are merely a click away and are available to even the most humble home.

We have the potential to write a page in history that has never before been written.

"Jewels" of Life

I* have painted exactly one painting in my life which hangs in my living room. It was the product of a 3-day painting workshop taught by a gifted artist, Jon McNaughton. Before attending, I had never picked up a paintbrush in my life. I never considered myself as having an artistic bone in my body; I just went to keep my artistic son company.

From the very beginning, Jon assured us we would be amazed at what we would create by the end of the third day. Trusting in him but doubting myself, I decided on a country garden scene at sunset. He guided us step by step, and the painting unfolded in layers. By

*Marlene

the end of the second day, I didn't have much more than a dark, scrambled mess of raw umber staring at me. Had I signed up by myself, I may not have returned for that third day because I was so embarrassed with my work. All along he kept assuring us to not give up; to trust him that magic on the third day was about to happen.

He was right. On the third and final day, he taught us about "jewels". Jewels were created by mixing white into various colors and applying them to key places on the painting. Suddenly the painting sprang to life and I found myself strolling on a little country pathway among the lilacs, iris and forget-me-nots. I felt the cool breezes of a summer evening and the comfort of the sunset's glow reflected in the windows of a country cottage. I couldn't stop looking at the painting because of the way it made me *feel*. I found it hard to believe that I had created this work of art, humble though it was. I marveled that something as simple as little "jewels" of light could give a painting such life and meaning.

A love of Beauty provides the "jewels" of life.

Making Good Use of the Harvest

Victor Frankl observed a small group of prisoners in those horrible death camps of Nazi Germany who secretly gathered together to recite poetry, sing songs and act in improvised plays even though such activities were forbidden and punishable by death. These "jewels" of life became so important to them that, he noticed they even skipped their meager meals at the end of grueling days of hard labor to allow more time to participate. Art and beauty became "the soul's weapon in the fight for self-preservation."[12]

The life sustaining power of beauty is found in its ability to inspire. To inspire implies filling with spirit or light. Dr. David Hawkins explains "the term 'spirit' refers to an unseen essence... this essence is vital; when we lose our spirit, we die—we *ex*pire from lack of that which *in*spires."[13]

When an individual or nation lacks in beauty and those qualities that we term "inspirational", he becomes "devoid of humanity, love and self-respect" and selfishness and violence fills in the void.

Making Good Use of the Harvest

It will be a challenge for many of us in our generation to awaken something in the hearts of our children that may even be asleep within us because of the world we have grown up in. An appreciation of beauty is emotional; it's a matter of the heart. We are a culture that has shifted to appealing to our minds and our senses. Our schools are textbook based which is an education of facts and information for the mind, not for the heart. There has been a major shift to secular and scientific critical thinking as well as a bombardment of sensual stimulation.

In the middle of winter, we are reminded that although the sun shines just as brightly in the winter as it does in the summer, without the sun's *warmth,* nothing grows. We need the intellect of the mind, but to grow as a people, we need the warmth of the heart as well. To crowd out the noise and become attuned to emotional responses can take time, but the efforts to do so are immensely satisfying.

Making Good Use of the Harvest

If of thy mortal goods thou art bereft,
And from thy slender store two loaves
alone to thee are left,
Sell one, and with the dole,
Buy hyacinths to feed thy soul.[14]

Our own personal search for Beauty is a journey we can share with our children and grandchildren. Helen Keller, who was blind and deaf, teaches us a lot about seeing. One day she was visited by a very dear friend who had just returned from a long walk in the woods. She asked what she had seen, to which she replied, "Nothing in particular."

Helen exclaimed, "I might have been incredulous had I not been accustomed to such responses for long ago I became convinced that the seeing see little. How was it possible, I asked myself, to walk for an hour through the woods and see nothing worthy of note? I who cannot see find hundreds of things to interest me through mere touch. I feel the delicate symmetry of a leaf. I pass my hands lovingly about the smooth skin of a silver birch, or the rough, shaggy bark of a pine. In spring I touch the branches of trees hopefully in search of a bud, the first sign of awakening Nature after her winter's sleep. I feel the delightful, velvety texture of a flower, and something of the miracle of Nature is revealed to me...

"At times my heart cries out with longing to see all these things. If I can get so much pleasure from mere touch, how much more beauty must be revealed by sight. Yet, those who have eyes apparently see little. The panorama of color and action which fills the world is taken for granted. It is human, perhaps, to appreciate little that which we have and to long for that which we have not, but it is a great pity that in the world of light, the gift of sight is used only as a mere convenience rather than as a means of adding fulness to life."[15]

Mothers can help their children "see" what most of the world cannot.

Making Good Use of the Harvest

The mother who covers her walls with great art that inspires souls, instead of paintings to match her couch; the mother who shares from her own heart beautiful words from the finest literature instead of empty words written merely to entertain; the mother who takes her child by the hand as she helps her child feel the stories and wonders of nature – this is the mother of poets and statesmen who will change the course of history.

Beauty, in many ways, has gone to sleep in our world. Nurturing our children's desire for and love of beauty in all its expressions is a truly restorative power in a Garden of Liberty. When there is a people who love beauty more than they love money, popularity or pleasure, they will create a light upon the hill that the nations of the earth, tired of the noxious thorns and briers, will once again look to and seek to emulate. Every effort to connect our children with that which is beautiful is some of the most important gardening work we will do.

Hope for a Bounteous Harvest

*"...an invisible power, greater than
the puny efforts of men, will fight for us..."*
– Abraham Lincoln

*"I would rather belong to a poor nation that was free than to a
rich nation that had ceased to be in love with liberty."*
– Woodrow Wilson

My* husband and I moved to Minnesota shortly after we were married. It was here that we moved into our first home. After moving in, we planted our first tree: it was a Marshal Ash. We planted it in the front yard, close to the street. I remember how fascinated we were with watching the tree grow. Every year we would care for and fertilize it. Each season, we would frequently take a yardstick out to measure the new growth. We would sit under the tree and enjoy the shade it provided.

*Tammy

Hope for a Bounteous Harvest

Then in the fall of 1991, after four years of watching our tree grow, Minnesota experienced what will be forever remembered as the "Halloween Blizzard." It was the first significant snowfall of the year, leaving 30" of snow within a twenty-four hour time period. The snow plows came through to clear the streets, leaving a large snow bank next to our curb and completely surrounding the base of our tree. The storm was followed by the "Thanksgiving Blizzard" that once again left record-breaking amounts of snow and added to an even larger snow bank around the base of the tree.

In Minnesota, winters are typically long and cold. The temperatures usually remain below freezing until the spring thaw. Consequently, the snow that had been dropped in those early snowstorms remained there until spring. After the driveway and sidewalk was clear, we accepted the large snow bank as a part of the front yard for the next several months. Our children enjoyed playing on them and watching the ever-increasing size of their sledding hill with each additional snowstorm.

Hope for a Bounteous Harvest

Then spring came, the snow melted and we discovered that some small animals had taken refuge from the cold at the base of the snow bank. The voles seemed to wreak havoc in many yards that year. The bark of our tree became the food supply for the winter for one family of voles. As we looked at the damage to the tree, we saw that it had been completely girdled. A ten-inch gap of bare trunk had been exposed. What did this mean for our tree?

As we researched, we learned that the nutrients flow just under the bark of the tree. The lifeline of the tree had been completely severed. The branches would not get the strength from the root, the leaves would soon wither, our shade would be lost, and our tree would eventually die.

We were left to question, is there anything that can be done to save our tree? We made phone calls to the local nurseries and county extension to see if there was anything we could do. We learned about a grafting procedure called a "bridge graft." We could cut last year's best growth off the ends of the branches and then graft them into the trunk at the top and bottom of the gap, creating a bridge for the nutrients to flow through. If the graft succeeded, the small branches would swell, creating new bark for the tree.

In our research we also learned that though the leaves were few in number, they played a critical role in healing. For these leaves collected energy from the sun to provide nourishment to the root.

My husband, Dale, devoted much time and effort as he carefully followed the instructions that had been given. He followed the grafting procedure with exactness. Then, we waited and watched. That year the leaves on our tree were very sparse. To the person just passing by, unaware of the stress that the tree was under, the few leaves were an indicator that the tree was dying. Some may prematurely determine that it would be best to cut it down and start over. Even the experts were skeptical about whether the procedure would work or not. But we remained hopeful.

Hope for a Bounteous Harvest

We loved our tree and didn't want to start over so we decided to make the tree's survival a matter of prayer. It was our faith that the Lord who is the creator of all things, and yet notices even a sparrow fall, would certainly be able to heal our tree. We patiently waited and prayed as time passed. The leaves were sparse for a couple of seasons. The strength remaining in the tree was used for healing. And then the first signs of new growth began to appear. It worked! It really worked! We felt so much gratitude as we watched the grafted branches swell. Eventually, the tree produced more leaves creating shade for us to enjoy. Once again, throughout the season we could measure the new growth.

Over the years the tree has continued to grow to full maturity. It is healthy and strong. The only indication that it ever struggled is a small scar that remains where the graft had taken place. A token reminder of the lessons learned and the reason our tree had survived.

Hope for a Bounteous Harvest

Liberty will endure

The cause of freedom has always been championed by the few and great things have often been accomplished by small and simple means. The ideas presented in this book are simple solutions to the seemingly never-ending sea of complex problems facing our nation today. In fact, they are so simple, they have been overlooked for decades. But please don't let the word *simple* fool you. These solutions *are* simple, but they are not easy. They require dedication, commitment, and consistency, but most of all they require a belief that they *will* work – that they will, in fact, solve our complex problems and not only *protect* liberty but *secure* it for generations to come.

We cannot allow fear to overcome us. Families have been deeply affected by the disturbing challenges of today. The economy that teeters on the verge of collapse has given rise to more financial burdens. We wonder how we'll make it through. Children are influenced by philosophies that run contrary to family traditions. Contentious rhetoric in our universities and news media create confusion and mistrust of leaders. Our Constitution is being shredded to pieces. Stories of shocking violence that have scrolled across TV screens in the past are now making their way into more and more neighborhoods. Many mothers have become fearful and anxious about the current trends and how those trends will affect their loved ones. We cannot completely protect our children, but we can prepare them to face whatever comes their way with their hope intact.

We are reminded of the anxiety and concern felt by another people in another place and time. The Apostle Paul lived in times of great uncertainty. Yet, even while confined to prison in Rome, he kept the faith and refused to succumb to fear. He admonished his fellow companions to do the same. In a letter to Timothy, one of his junior companions, he offered strength and encouragement. First, Paul reminded Timothy of the faith of his mother and grandmother and then explained that fear does not come from God. Paul writes:

Hope for a Bounteous Harvest

"Wherefore I put thee in remembrance that thou stir up the gift of God, which is in thee...For God hath not given us the spirit of fear; but of power, and of love, and of a sound mind."[16]

Who among us can say that he or she has not felt fear? Fears have increased as groups of men and women try to stand up for their beliefs. Some groups have been attacked more than others in the battle of ideas regarding the future of our country. We see a growing sense of discouragement and capitulation among the masses. As Timothy of old, we too must remember the faith of earlier generations and recognize that fear does not come from God.

Today, we find mothers who suffer from the fear of ridicule, the fear of failure, the fear of ignorance, and the fear of the future. To them we say, "For God hath not given us the spirit of fear; but of power, and of love, and of a sound mind."

Hope for a Bounteous Harvest

The principles discussed in this book are the great antidotes to the fears that rob mothers of their strength and sometimes knock them down to defeat. These are principles of power–the power of faith, the power of virtue and the power of patriotism founded in correct knowledge and truth. Restore a love of God, a love of Goodness and a love of Country and you will restore liberty to our great nation for those are the three pillars upon which freedom rests. We are reminded of these pillars in our flag: the white stars on a blue background are a call to remember Heaven's guiding and protective Hand, the white stripes call to our minds purity and virtue and the stripes of red cause us to think of the blood spilled in our behalf in the cause of freedom and love of country. Even Josef Stalin, an enemy to freedom, recognized the source of America's strength: "America is like a healthy body and its resistance is threefold: its Patriotism, its Morality, and its Spiritualism."

Mothers clothed in power, love and sound minds can bridge the chasm of fear and change the course of the nation. An influential leader of a young women's organization described it well when she said:

"The world has enough women who are tough; we need women who are tender. There are enough women who are coarse. We need women who are kind. There are enough women who are rude; we need women who are refined. We have enough women of fame and fortune; we need more women of faith. We have enough greed. We need more goodness. We have enough vanity, we need more virtue. We have enough popularity, we need more purity."[17]

Rose Wilder Lane, the daughter of Laura Ingalls Wilder, was a voice for freedom. For a time, she sided with Communist thinking as the answer for alleviating human suffering and want. In theory, it seemed practical and reasonable – until she lived abroad and saw with her own eyes the theory in action. When she returned home, her writings during the Great Depression and the war that followed shined a 100 watt, non-energy saving floodlight on the cause of and critical need for freedom.

Hope for a Bounteous Harvest

America was going through dark days, like we are now, when she wrote the following:

"In Des Moines, I listened while eight influential businessmen discussed facts. Congress had abdicated. The federal executive power, by decree, was looting the banks; bankers were silent. Political power, consolidated and unrestrained, was wrecking the American political structure. Civil law no longer protected human rights. They said, "There is no refuge. We had the only protection for human rights on the earth, and it is gone. The world will go back to the Dark Ages."

I said, "How can you men know this, and do nothing? Is this possible? You know that our country is being destroyed, and you do nothing to save it? You actually understand that your own property, your liberty, your lives, are in danger and you do nothing?"

"That's it," they said.

Hope for a Bounteous Harvest

"It was a nightmare. When I found anyone who understood the situation as I did, he had no hope, and pessimism itself is not American. Americans hold the truths that all men are born equal and endowed by their Creator with inalienable liberty. Freedom is the nature of men, every person is self-controlling and himself responsible for his thoughts, his speech, his acts. This is a fact; we know it. Americans established the Republic upon that fact.

My friends said, "There's no use, nothing can be done. Americans don't want liberty any more."

The answer to that is, "Do you? What are YOU doing to defend your liberty?"

They replied wearily, . . . "An individual is nothing. You can't resist history."

"Resist history?" I said. "You and I make history. History is nothing whatever but a record of what

living persons have done in the past. Americans make history and America is not dead."[18]

It *is* late but it is not *too* late. Please join with other Gardeners of Liberty who have taken a stand *for* freedom as we write a new chapter in American history – the chapter where we secure the blessings of liberty for ourselves and our posterity. The rallying words of Washington, America's first general in the fight for freedom, echo through time to us who are engaged in the battle today:

"...the time is near at hand, which will determine whether Americans are to be freemen. The fate of unknown millions will depend, under God, on the courage and conduct of this army. Let us rely on the goodness of our cause, and the aid of the Supreme Being, in whose hands victory is, to animate and encourage us to great and noble actions."

A wise man posed the question:

Hope for a Bounteous Harvest

"When the real history of mankind is fully disclosed, will it feature the echoes of gunfire or the shaping sound of lullabies? The great armistices made by military men or the peacemaking of women in homes and in neighborhoods? Will what happened in cradles and kitchens prove to be more controlling than what happened in congresses?"[19]

We answer with a resounding YES! Truly, through the power of love, "the hand that rocks the cradle will rule the nations"[20] and we'll once again enjoy the bounteous harvest of a beautiful Garden of Liberty.

Gardening Tools for Gardeners of Liberty

(You can find these at gardenofliberty.org)

American Heritage Center

This is available free online and contains a wealth of resources, support and encouragement to instill a love of country and deep appreciation for America's heritage and Constitution.

Freedom Series

Preserve America's story the way it used to be told. The Freedom Series is twelve volumes of stories drawn from literature written for young people before 1923; a golden age when the writings were filled with faith, virtue and patriotism. These books provide a perfect introduction to history and have something for every age group to read silently, read together or to retell from the heart.

Lessons in Liberty

The principles of liberty do not come instinctively; they must be taught. An excellent starting place is *The 5000 Year Leap,* which gives you 28 principles of freedom to discuss as families. We provide companion resource guides to go along with the Freedom Series that highlight these 28 principles for further conversation. We also promote programs for learning to know and love our Constitution.

Liberty Vine Newsletter

This is our free monthly newsletter which provides an avenue for mothers to share ideas and successes. Topics include good books to read, kids' activity ideas, relevant issues and even homemaking tips such as making family dinner hour possible because, as Ronald Reagan said, "all great change in America begins at the dinner table."

For Book Lovers

As mothers restore the family library as the most inviting room in the home and stock it full of the best books, we'll see a stronger generation emerge. We accept the convenience of digital media but value the importance of physically preserving the best literature in our homes. You will find a wealth of book suggestions.

Storytellers Corner

We encourage mothers to put the books down and tell stories from the heart. Nothing else has a more powerful influence. We offer training in the art of storytelling drawn from writings during America's revival in the art a hundred years ago as well as a treasury of stories to tell "by heart"; stories to instill a love of God, a love of Goodness, a love of Country and a love of Beauty.

Story Bible

Helping our children love the Bible from infancy is vital to securing freedom. This Story Bible is perfect for family read-aloud time. It contains over 400 stories from the Bible in the language of the of the King James version.

15 Minute Mind Workout

"If we mean to have heroes, statesmen and philosophers, we should have learned women." (Abigail Adams) A mother whose mind and heart is stored with great and noble thoughts naturally passes those thoughts along to her children. We take time to exercise our bodies. We need to take time to exercise and stretch our minds. This is a national challenge of self-education based in the Harvard Classics.

Future Dreams

Conferences and Workshops

We look forward to gathering mothers and mothers-at-heart where they can feel strength and support and feel inspired by speakers who will help them fill their critical role in preserving freedom.

Education for a Free People

Our current compulsory system of education is not conducive to a free people. We believe it's time for a new model of education based on the principles that all true education is self-education. Our children need to know more than how to make a living – they need to know how to make a life. We seek to provide a lab where new educational ideas outside the mainstream can be explored.

American Heritage in Art and Music

We would like to provide a venue for artists to create new masterpieces to remind our children of our national heritage — masterpieces that can be hung on walls in homes across America. We also seek to reacquaint a new generation with our folk songs so they can sing songs straight from the heart of America.

A Gardener of Liberty:

--values the God-given right to self-governance and choice

--understands that freedom is a rare and prized possession

--knows the price of freedom is constant care and vigilance

--recognizes that knowing how to live as a free people does not come instinctively; principles of freedom must be studied and applied

--instills a love of our heritage and lessons in liberty in the next generation of gardeners

--places the heart of the individual above the mind of the masses

--relies on the Hand of Divine Providence

Are you a Gardener of Liberty?

Join us at gardenofliberty.org.

Endnotes

1. Herbert Kaufman, "The Dreamers", *More Heart Throbs* [New York: Grosset and Dunlap, 1911] p. 350.

2. Sheri Dew, " The Influence of Mothers, *Deseret News*, May 8, 2011.

3. E.T. Sullivan, "God's Way," The Treasure Chest [New York: Harper and Rowe, 1965] p.53.

4. George B. Cheever, *Right of the Bible in our Public Schools*, [New York: Robert Carter and Brothers, 1854] p. 277.

5. ibid.

6. David Starr Jordan, *The Care and Culture of Men*, [San Francisco: Whitaker & Ray-Wiggin Co., 1896] p. 57.

7. ibid.

8. *The Holy Bible*, Amos 8:13

9. Louise Seymour Houghton, *Telling Bible Stories*, [New York: Charles Scribner's Sons, 1916] pp. 8-9.

Endnotes

10. Adapted from Thomas Sowell's "Does Patriotism Matter?" *Deseret News*, July 3, 2008.

11. *The Singing Revolution*, a documentary, singingrevolution.com

12. William Nixon, " The Art of Truth", *Latter-day Digest*, December 1993, pp. 9-19.

13. Dr. David Hawkins, *Power vs. Force*, [New York: Hay House, 2002]

14. Moslih Eddin Saadi

15. Helen Keller, "Three Days to See", *Story Biographies*, [New York: Harcourt Brace, 1936]

16. *The Holy Bible*, 2 Timothy 1:6-7

17. Margaret Nadauld, "The Joy of Womanhood", *Ensign*, November 2000.

18. Rose Wilder Lane, "Credo", *Saturday Evening Post*, 1936. (Later published as a booklet, "Give Me Liberty") http://www.panarchy.org/lane/liberty.html

19. Neal A. Maxwell, *Ensign*, May 1978, pp. 10-11.

20. William Ross Wallace, "The Hand that Rocks the
Cradle is the Hand that Rules the World" first published in
1865:

Blessings on the hand of women!
Angels guard its strength and grace,
In the palace, cottage, hovel,
Oh, no matter where the place;
Would that never storms assailed it,
Rainbows ever gently curled;
For the hand that rocks the cradle
Is the hand that rules the world.

Infancy's the tender fountain,
Power may with beauty flow,
Mother's first to guide the streamlets,
From them souls unresting grow—
Grow on for the good or evil,
Sunshine streamed or evil hurled;
For the hand that rocks the cradle
Is the hand that rules the world.

Woman, how divine your mission
Here upon our natal sod!
Keep, oh, keep the young heart open
Always to the breath of God!
All true trophies of the ages
Are from mother-love impearled;
For the hand that rocks the cradle
Is the hand that rules the world.

Blessings on the hand of women!
Fathers, sons, and daughters cry,
And the sacred song is mingled
With the worship in the sky–
Mingles where no tempest darkens,
Rainbows evermore are hurled;
For the hand that rocks the cradle
Is the hand that rules the world.

HomeMakers for America
National Executive Board
(and co-authors of this book)

Kimberly Fletcher is the founder and president of HomeMakers for America. Kimberly comes from a long line of freedom loving patriots including several who served in the Revolutionary War. She has a deep love and affection for her country and believes the best color in the world is red, white, and blue! She is an Air Force wife and mother of eight children.

Marlene Peterson serves as Vice-President of HFA. Marlene strongly believes in the power of stories; that our children's ability to maintain hope in the days ahead will be in direct proportion to how broad and how deep their reservoir of stories is. Her passion is finding and sharing stories from yesteryear. She and her husband, Brent, have raised eight daughters and one son and are thoroughly enjoying their grandchildren.

Tammy Hulse serves as second Vice-President of HFA. Tammy's passion is empowering people with the truth. She is dedicated to teaching the truth about our country's history and Constitution, the importance of families and the significant role of the homemaker and mother. She and her husband, Dale, have raised three sons and four daughters.

We do not need more material development
we need more spiritual development.
We do not need more intellectual power,
we need more moral power.
We do not need more knowledge,
we need more character.
We do not need more government,
we need more culture.
We do not need more law,
we need more religion.
We do not need more of the things that are seen,
we need more of the things that are unseen.

It is on that side of life that it is desirable
to put the emphasis at this present time.
If that side is strengthened,
the other side will take care of itself.

It is that side which is
the foundation of all else.
If the foundation be firm,
the superstructure will stand.

--Calvin Coolidge

home♥makers
F O R   A M E R I C A
. . . gardeners of liberty